THE MILITARY EXPERIENCE.

Special Operations:
WEAPONS

THE MILITARY EXPERIENCE.

Special Operations:
WEAPONS

DON NARDO

MORGAN REYNOLDS
PUBLISHING

GREENSBORO, NORTH CAROLINA

The Military Experience.
Special Operations: Weapons
Copyright © 2013 by Morgan Reynolds Publishing

Library of Congress Cataloging-in-Publication Data

Nardo, Don, 1947-
 Special operations : weapons / by Don Nardo.
    p. cm. -- (The military experience)
 Includes bibliographical references.
 ISBN 978-1-59935-358-6 -- ISBN 978-1-59935-359-3 (e-book) 1.
Special
forces (Military science)--United States--Equipment and supplies. 2.
Military weapons--United States. I. Title.
 U262.N37 2013
 356'.16--dc23

                          2012017100

Printed in the United States of America
First Edition

Book cover and interior designed by:
Ed Morgan, navyblue design studio
Greensboro, NC

Table of Contents

A Basic Underwater Demolition/ SEAL (BUD/S) student wades ashore on San Clemente Island, off the coast of California, during an exercise.

Lance Corporal Osvaldo J. Lopez keeps his combat skills honed. The twenty-two-year-old from Bayonne, New Jersey, is a rifleman with the 2nd Battalion, 2nd Marine Regiment.

CHAPTER ONE

DEADLY
Handheld
WEAPONS

One of the most violent and scary days in Master Sergeant Steve Rainey's life was April 7, 2003. Back then he was leader of a unit of the U.S. Army's Special Forces, sometimes called the Green Berets. There were twelve men in the group. Each was a superbly trained commando, or "special ops" fighter. The Special Forces are the Army's version of the Navy's famous SEAL units. Members of these groups carry out missions that are too difficult for ordinary soldiers.

DEATHTRAP IN IRAQ

It was just such a mission that Rainey undertook on that day in 2003. The U.S. military had recently attacked Iraq. That Middle Eastern nation was believed to possess weapons of mass destruction, and the United States and its allies felt they had to disarm the Iraqis. Rainey's orders were to go to the small town of Abbas. A high-placed Iraqi official was hiding there and needed to be captured.

Rainey knew that Abbas was crawling with enemy soldiers. So to go in with a large force of men, guns blazing, would ignite a major battle. While it was raging, the target would have plenty of time to escape. It made more sense to sneak in with a few well-trained fighters. For this job Rainey selected six of the men from his unit.

The team went quietly into Abbas on April 7 as planned. They found the house where the Iraqi official was hiding, and they seized and cuffed him. But when they were about to leave, gunfire erupted. Rainey and his men dove for cover behind their vehicles. Scanning the area, they saw that dozens of Iraqis had surrounded them. A hail of bullets from the enemy soldiers' machine guns sprayed the vehicles. The special ops fighters were trapped in what military experts call a "kill box." It means a place with no way out—a deathtrap.

Rainey and his men were trained not to panic, however, and they swung into action. Some of them used their trusty M4 carbines to return fire. Meanwhile, the others grabbed weapons more powerful than those wielded by the Iraqis. These included M240 machine guns and an MK19 grenade launcher. Bullets poured from them and battered the enemy positions. Hastily loading up the vehicles, the commandos jumped in and sped down the street. "Rainey followed on foot, still firing," an expert observer later reported. "Once they were out of the kill box, [he] hopped into . . . one of the [vehicles] and they took off!"

Lance Corporal Kendall S. Boyd (*left*) and Private First Class Ryan J. Jones (*right*), combat engineer, Combat Assault Battalion, 3rd Marine Division, hone their machine gunnery skills by firing the M240G medium machine gun while at Camp Hansen in Okinawa, Japan.

THE M4 AND M9

Rainey and his men survived partly because of their excellent training and skills. But the fire power of their weapons played a big part, too. Almost all were handheld. Since the dawn of warfare thousands of years ago, soldiers have relied mostly on weapons they could carry themselves. At first these were rocks and clubs. Spears, swords, and the bow and arrow followed. And finally came guns, or firearms, including one-handed pistols and two-handed rifles.

fact BOX

Sniper Rifles

Almost all U.S. special ops fighters learn to used sniper rifles. The leading sniper rifle among them is the M24. It weighs a bit more than 15 pounds (6.8 kg) and can fire bullets accurately up to 1,500 feet (457 m), almost a third of a mile.

M24 rifle

Today's special ops fighters use highly advanced kinds of handheld fire-arms. The Army Special Forces and Navy SEALs are only two of several existing groups of U.S. military commandos. Among the others are the Army's Rangers and Delta Force and the Air Force's Combat Control Teams and Pararescuemen, or PJs. Members of these various special ops branches often have their personal favorite weapons. But all are trained to use a few standard ones.

One of these standard firearms is the M4 carbine assault rifle. It shoots between 700 and 950 rounds, or bullets, per minute. These rounds travel at an incredible speed—more than 2,000 feet per second. So they can rip apart the wall of an average house, not to mention a human body. For a weapon that does so much damage, the M4 is surprisingly compact and light. It weighs roughly 7 pounds (around 3 kg) and is easy to carry.

A shell casing flies out with a trail of smoke as U.S. Army Private First Class Michael Freise fires an M4 rifle during a reflex firing exercise at the Rodriguez Live Fire Complex, in the Republic of Korea.

Aviation Electronics Technician 2nd Class Filipe Teixeira looks over his results after participating in M4 service rifle qualifications at Joint Expeditionary Base Little Creek-Fort Story, in Virginia Beach, Virginia.

Many commandos carry a pistol, too, in case their rifle fails for some reason. Among the most popular pistols is the M9 Beretta. It's small but powerful. Also, it fires quite a few rounds before needing to be reloaded. Its magazine, or clip, holds fifteen bullets.

M9 Beretta

HUMANS AND HARDWARE

Along with their rifles and pistols, U.S. commandos employ somewhat heavier handheld firearms. Chief among these are various types of machine guns. The M240, which Steve Rainey and his men used effectively in Iraq, has a greater range than the M4 carbine. The M240 also fires a heavier bullet, making it more destructive. Some special ops fighters prefer a similar machine gun, the M249. They like the fact that it fires the same size bullets as the M4. That way they have to carry only one kind of ammo (short for ammunition).

Modern commandos have developed a special bond with these and other deadly weapons. In a very real way, they can't function without each other. Special ops fighters have an old saying that goes, "Humans are more important than hardware . . . but the humans need their hardware to fight."

Soldier with an M240

Better Than the M4?

HK416

According to unnamed sources within the U.S. military, some members of the elite Army Delta Force became dissatisfied with their M4 carbines. The problem was that in desert areas sand got inside their rifles. So a new rifle was made for them—the HK416. It looks and operates much like the M4. However, it is better than the M4 because sand and dust don't get inside so easily. It appears that some of the Navy's SEALs liked the HK416 and started using it. According to another unnamed military source, the SEALs who killed Osama bin Laden in 2011 were carrying HK416s.

Explosive Ordnance Disposal (EOD) technicians explode or "cook off" old ammunition and ordnance that is no longer usable, in Kuwait. EOD technicians use C4 Plastic explosive charges to completely destroy the weapons. EOD teams from the U.S. Army, Navy, Air Force, and coalition forces conduct training exercises to improve joint capabilities between the services.

CHAPTER TWO

Devices That Go BOOM!

Besides their personal firearms, almost all U.S. commandos are trained to use heavier, even more lethal weapons. In general, these more destructive war tools create explosions of varying size. So one can jokingly but fairly accurately call them devices that go boom.

SIMPLE BUT VERY DAMAGING

These explosive weapons are no joke for enemy forces, however. U.S. special ops warriors use them to destroy enemy houses, cars, jeeps, and even tanks. And any human beings on the receiving end of such devices have nearly zero chance of survival.

Even the smallest and simplest of these weapons—the grenade— does serious damage. All U.S. commandos learn to use grenades. As former Air Force sergeant and weapons expert Rod Powers puts it, they "are nothing more than small bombs, containing explosives or chemicals." The most common type is the M67 fragmentation gre- nade. When it explodes, it scatters tiny metal particles in all direc- tions. The zone of death or serious injury for the weapon is about 50 feet (15 m). Other grenades spray fire, smoke, tear gas, or deadly chemicals.

Dummy hand grenades used for practice

Grenades can be thrown by hand, in which case they are called "hand grenades." An average commando can hurl a grenade at least 130 feet (40 m). Special ops fighters also fire grenades from special devices. Appropriately, they are called "grenade launchers." The Army Rangers and some other special ops groups use the M203 grenade launcher. It is lightweight and fits neatly under the barrel of a rifle. The M203 can send a grenade hurtling more than 330 feet (101 m) to a target.

A U.S. soldier holds an M203 grenade launcher.

Another grenade launcher used by U.S. commandos is heavier, more powerful, and hence more destructive. The awesome MK19 is a grenade-launching machine gun. It weighs a little more than 72 pounds (33 kg). A person can place it on a stand to fire it from the ground or mount it on a truck or other vehicle. According to an official Army Web site, the MK19 is "designed to deliver decisive firepower against enemy [soldiers] and lightly armored vehicles." So special ops fighters use it when much larger forces of enemy soldiers and vehicles are closing in on them. Those bigger forces can be rapidly reduced to rubble by a couple of MK19s. This is because the weapon can fire a frightening sixty grenades per minute, or one grenade every second.

Soldiers with an MK19 grenade launcher

MK19

fact BOX

The Original MK19

The MK19 was originally created for U.S. Navy fighters in the Vietnam War. They used it to fire grenades from river patrol boats into the nearby forests, where enemy soldiers were firing on them.

AMAZING FIREPOWER

Navy SEALs, Army Rangers, members of Army Delta Force, and some other U.S. commandos also receive training in small missile systems. These extremely lethal weapons have amazing firepower. They are designed to take out enemy tanks and armored vehicles. Moreover, some of them can be fired from positions miles from a target. That makes it less risky for the person or persons firing them.

Of these missile systems, one of the more impressive and effective is the TOW. These letters stand for a real mouthful of military jargon: Tube-launched, Optically tracked, Wire command-link guided missile. The wallop this weapon delivers is even bigger than its name. The TOW can penetrate and destroy most armored vehicles. It can shatter houses and other small buildings as well.

That huge destructive power is crammed into a shockingly small package. A TOW missile is only 46 inches (117 cm) long, about the size of four footballs placed end-to-end. It weighs just 47 pounds (21 kg). Its small size and weight gives it an enormous range. When fired, the missile can fly up to 12,290 feet (3,750 m), or well more than 2 miles (3.2 km).

Using a tripod-mounted BGM-71 TOW, an antitank missile, U.S. Army Private First Class David Mitchell scans the landscape surrounding Vehicle Patrol Base Badel at the mouth of the Narang Valley in Konar province, Afghanistan, in May 2009.

A soldier launches an FGM-148 Javelin antitank missile.

Many special ops fighters also know how to use an antitank missile system called Javelin. It first appeared in 1996. A Javelin missile is 3 feet, 6 inches (1 m) long and weighs 50 pounds (23 kg). It can destroy tanks up to 8,200 feet (2,500 m), or more than a mile and a half, away. One big advantage of the Javelin is that a commando can fire it from his shoulder.

Another small, shoulder-fired missile used by special ops fighters is the FIM-9 Stinger. Its job is to shoot down low-flying aircraft like helicopters. "The Stinger is a true 'fire and forget' missile," Powers explains. It requires "no inputs from the gunner once the weapon is fired. This allows the gunner to take cover, move to an alternate position, or engage additional targets."

Clearly, U.S. commandos have a major arsenal of powerful weapons at their disposal. Plus, many of these fighters have the training to use them all. If properly equipped, five or six of them could devastate hundreds of enemy soldiers with ordinary training and weapons.

True EXPLOSIVES Experts

Many of the weapons used by U.S. special ops fighters allow them to destroy or kill from great distances. Sometimes, however, they need to demolish targets at close range. This often requires planting explosives directly onto selected targets. Members of the Army's Rangers and Special Forces have blown up many bridges this way. And Navy SEALs have sunk a number of enemy ships by attaching explosives to the undersides of their hulls. Many of these commandos become true explosives experts. The most common substance they employ is C4, also called plastique. With a texture similar to clay, it can be molded into any desired shape. Another advantage is that it is safe to use. It does not explode when exposed to flame or a gunshot. Only when the commando flips the switch of a remote detonator does the C4 ignite and do its deadly job.

Private First Class Laura Mellinger inserts blasting caps into blocks of C4 explosives.

CHAPTER THREE

Valuable
CLOSE AIR
SUPPORT

An MC-130P Combat Shadow refuels an HH-60 Pave Hawk helicopter from the 33rd Rescue Squadron. The refueling mission is in support of operations after a severe earthquake in Japan, in 2011.

U.S. special ops fighters train hard for their secret missions. To perform those operations, they must first get to their targets, which can be anywhere in the world. For that task, the military provides special aircraft. They include both airplanes and helicopters, as well as a craft that combines elements of both.

These flying weapons systems also provide various sorts of aid to the commandos once they are on the ground. They fight off or destroy enemy forces that threaten the fighters, for example. Or they drop vital supplies to the commandos. Later, when the mission is complete, they may pick up the fighters and ferry them home. Together, these and other crucial tasks these craft perform are called "close air support."

The special craft that provide this support are stationed at bases in different parts of the country. One of the main hubs is the U.S. Air Force Special Operations Command (AFSOC) at Hurlburt Field, near Fort Walton Beach, Florida. It is home base for several of the flying fortresses that back up the Army's and Navy's special ops units. These include the Rangers, Delta Force, and Navy SEALs, among others.

A CV-22 Osprey aircraft from the 8th Special Operations Squadron flies over the Emerald Coast outside Hurlburt Field, Florida. While over the water, the crew practiced using a hoist, which is used to rescue stranded personnel.

THE VERSATILE TALON GUNSHIP

Members of Delta Force, for instance, have flown behind enemy lines in the MC-130 Combat Talon II gunship. This versatile plane is equipped with the highest quality radar. It also has devices that can jam, or obstruct, enemy communications. This allows the plane to fly in and out of enemy territory without being detected. It inserts, or places, commandos near a target in two ways. One is to land in the area. The other is to fly over and let the men parachute in.

Two MC-130 Talons secretly inserted a group of Navy SEALs into Afghanistan not long after the September 11, 2001, attacks. One of these commandos later vividly recalled the amazing accuracy achieved by the planes and their pilots:

> The pilots took [the planes] down to a few hundred feet. At that height, the MC-130s fly themselves with their terrain-following radar, and if the ground is hilly, it can get really rough [for the passengers] in the back. . . . I can't say enough [good things] about our special operations pilots. They made a straight pass in and dropped us right onto the insertion point.

Soldiers with the 2nd Commando Regiment, an Australian Army Special Forces unit, jump from a U.S. Air Force MC-130 transport aircraft during an exercise over the Great Barrier Reef in Australia, in 2011.

An MC-130H Combat Talon II from the 1st Special Operations Squadron flies a training mission during an exercise in Bangladesh, a country in South Asia.

In addition, the Talon features STAR, the Surface To Air Recovery system. This astonishing tool allows the craft to scoop up a person on the ground without landing. The person dons a special protective suit with a strong lifeline attached to it. On the line's other end is a helium-filled balloon. The balloon rises and floats in the air. And as the plane comes zooming by at 150 miles (241 km) per hour, it grabs hold of the floating line. With a big yank, the line goes taut and lifts the person upward. Then a machine aboard the plane reels him upward and inside. One important use for STAR is recovering commandos in dangerous areas in which a plane can't safely land.

A SPOOKY AIRCRAFT

Another valuable AFSOC gunship is the AC-130 Spectre, which military personnel playfully call "Spooky." (The word *Spectre* means "ghost.") Like the Talon gunship, Spooky can insert commandos into a target area via parachute. The jumps are of two principal kinds. One is called HALO, which stands for "High-Altitude, Low-Opening." In other words, the special ops fighters leave the plane at a high altitude, usually 32,000 feet (10,000 m). They do not open their chutes right away. Rather, they wait until they reach 2,500 feet (760 m). This approach allows them to get to the ground fast, so there is less chance the enemy will notice them.

The other kind of jump is called HAHO, or "High-Altitude, High-Opening." Here, the men jump at 32,000 feet and open their chutes after only nine or ten seconds. It takes them up to eighty minutes to reach the ground. The point is to jump while outside of enemy territory and drift steadily inside while descending. Local radar cannot detect them.

The Spooky gunship can also support ground forces using its large array of weapons. Among them are two Vulcan cannons that fire powerful projectiles at the rate of 2,500 rounds per minute. One of the craft's finest moments came in 1989. The United States conducted a police action in Panama, in Central America. Special ops fighters were heavily involved, along with regular soldiers. The AC-130 Spectre provided outstanding close air support. Rod Powers recalls, "As the only close air support platform in the [conflict], Spectres were credited with saving the lives of many [U.S.] personnel."

An AC-130H gunship flies over
Hurlburt Field, in Florida.

SOC HELICOPTERS

In addition to its airplane gunships, the AFSOC operates several types of helicopters. The best-known is the UH-60 Black Hawk. This is because it was the subject of the 2001 film, *Black Hawk Down*. The movie told the true story of an incident in the African nation of Somalia in 1993. Two Black Hawks were shot down, and two American commandos died. The Black Hawk often flies low over enemy terrain at 90 miles (140 km) per hour. It can insert or evacuate eleven commandos at a time.

UH-60 Black Hawk

V-22B Osprey

fact
BOX

The Peculiar V-22B Osprey

Many U.S. commandos are now transported by the
V-22B Osprey. As aircraft go, it is very peculiar. This is
because it flies like a plane but lands vertically like a
helicopter. In 2008, the V-22B replaced the AFSOC's
Pave Low copter, which had been in service for some
forty years.

CHAPTER FOUR

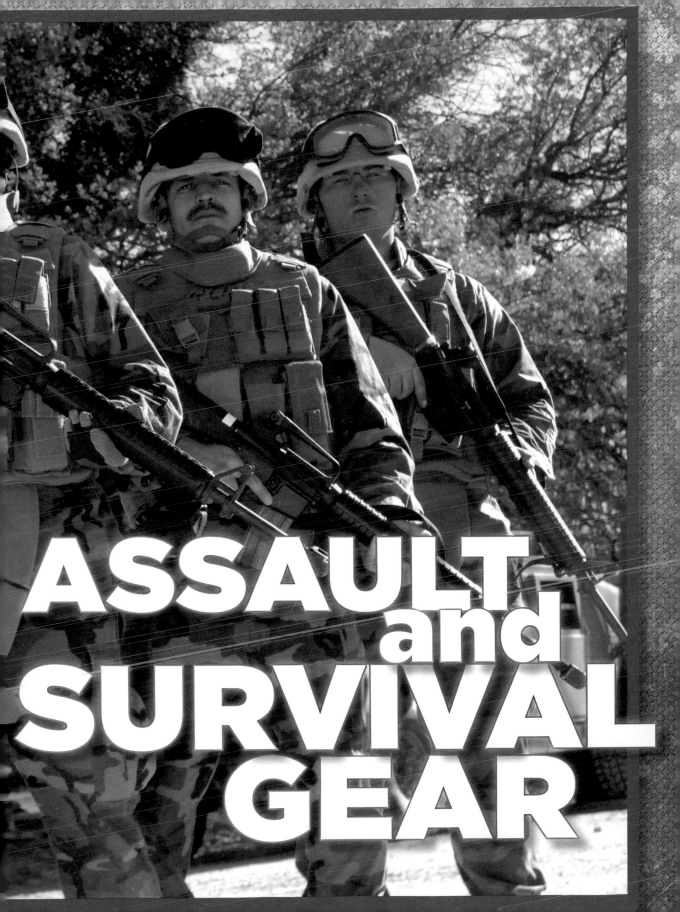

ASSAULT and SURVIVAL GEAR

Members of the U.S. commando units know that it takes more than transport planes to get them to their targets. They must also carry with them various kinds of assault and survival gear. These are tools, devices, and gadgets that first allow them to survive during the mission. Second, these tools allow the fighters to overcome obstacles in the path to the target.

That path might lead through a dense jungle or desert wilderness. Such situations require navigation equipment, the more advanced the better. The path may also be blocked by watery or mountainous barriers. So the commandos would need scuba or climbing gear. Such devices can be thought of as secondary weapons in the struggle to complete the mission.

DRESSING FOR THE JOB

One of the most potent of these tools is camouflage. It consists of a fighter trying to blend as much as possible with his natural surroundings. Commandos often find themselves in situations where it is vital to remain unseen by the enemy. That goal is hard to achieve without camouflage, or "camo" as special ops fighters often call it.

The most common type of camouflage employed by commandos revolves around their outfits. Most standard military uniforms are made of material of a single color. In contrast, the clothing worn on special ops missions is multicolored. An observer explains:

> Camouflage material is colored with dull hues that match the predominant colors of the surrounding environment. In jungle warfare, camouflage is typically green and brown, to match the forest foliage and dirt. In the desert, military forces use a range of tan colors. Camouflage for snowy climates is colored with whites and grays. To complete the concealment, soldiers paint their face with colors matching the camouflage material.

Private First Class Joel Graham of B Battery, 1st Battalion, 377th Field Artillery Regiment (Air Assault), Fort Bragg, North Carolina, puts on camouflage paint as his unit prepares to board the ship that will take him to Vieques Island, Puerto Rico, for a joint exercise with Marines.

For a commando, another aspect of dressing for the job is wearing clothing that protects him from harm. To this end, special ops warriors sometimes wear armored vests. Like those worn by regular Army soldiers, they are often made of Kevlar. It is a human-made fiber five times stronger than steel. That makes it tough enough to resist bullets from a number of small firearms.

Soldiers check their course with compasses during a foot patrol while training at Camp Atterbury Joint Maneuver Training Center in Edinburgh, Indiana.

FROM FINDING ONE'S WAY TO SEEING IN THE DARK

Other critical tools modern commandos commonly use in the field help them find their way or overcome obstacles. Finding their way includes determining both their present location and the exact location of the mission target. This job can be accomplished partly with detailed maps and a compass they carry in their pack. But in recent years commandos have come to rely on GPS, or the Global Positioning System. In his book about special ops forces, Fred J. Pushies tells how "GPS uses a collection of satellites that orbit the Earth twice daily. During this orbiting they transmit precise time, latitude, longitude, and altitude information. Using a GPS receiver, special operations forces can [find] their exact location anywhere on Earth."

Among the many obstacles that special ops fighters encounter on missions are steep or vertical barriers. These range from cliff faces to the sides of buildings. The men surmount such barriers using simple but strong climbing and rappelling gear. These include nylon ropes and metal pitons (the bolts that anchor them to the barrier's surface).

Other obstacles the commandos may run into hinder their breathing or vision. If the air suddenly becomes thick with dust or smoke, they can slip on a lightweight gas mask. It filters out the unclean air long enough for the fighter to reach a safer area.

Similarly, when night descends, limiting what can be seen, a commando can don a set of night vision goggles. They allow the wearer quite literally to see in the dark. A noted military observer says, "The devices are sensitive to a broad spectrum of light, from visible through [normally invisible] infrared. [They] increase the light available at the infrared end of the spectrum by casting a beam of light that is not visible to the human eye . . . giving the [commando] the ability to operate with little or no illumination from the moon [or] stars."

These and other survival and assault tools give American special ops fighters an edge in dangerous situations. Maintaining that edge is crucial. It can make the difference between success and failure, or between life and death.

A U.S. Army soldier lays down suppressive fire during a raid in Al Jaff, a mock city at the National Training Center at Fort Irwin, California.

A STRICT CODE of HONOR

U.S. commandos protect themselves with all manner of devices. They include rifles, pistols, grenades, camouflage, and bullet-proof vests. One other shield they rely on is not material in nature, however. Rather, it is psychological or spiritual and builds confidence and character. It consists of living and fighting by a strict code of honor. Some have put that code into words. The Army's Green Berets, for example, have a creed that says:

> I am an American Special Forces soldier. A Professional! I will do all that my nation requires of me. I pledge to uphold the honor and integrity of all I am—in all I do. I will keep my mind and body clean, alert and strong, for this is my debt to those who depend on me.

Special Forces Green Beret soldiers at
Arlington National Cemetery

fact
BOX

Portable Power Sources

One of the more recent developments in special
tools and gear for commandos are portable solar
panels. They are small, lightweight, and fold up
into a compact carrying case. With them, a special
ops fighter can charge his cell phone and other
electronic devices while in the field.

CHAPTER FIVE

SPECIAL OPS WEAPONS in ACTION

A U.S. Marine dashes over foothills and trenches while conducting a mission in support of Operation Iraqi Freedom in Iraq.

Any U.S. commando will confirm that no two special ops missions are alike. So the exact weapons and equipment used will also differ. Still, certain basic weapons and gear are fairly common to most special ops missions. Nearly all commandos carry one or more handheld firearms during missions, for example. Also, most wear protective Kevlar vests and/or helmets. And a majority of missions involve some sort of close air support. Their value becomes clearer when one examines how they were used in a real-life mission.

LIGHTNING BOLTS FROM THE GODS

One of the better-known missions involving special ops fighters was the 1989 U.S. invasion of Panama. American officials cited several reasons for this police action. Among them was that Panamanian military officer Manuel Noriega had recently seized power. He had set up a criminal operation. And one major aim of the mission was to capture Noriega and restore democracy to Panama.

The plans for the mission, called Operation Just Cause, called for inserting numerous commandos into Panama. They included members of the Army's Rangers and Green Berets. There were also a number of Navy SEALs and Air Force special operations personnel. Some were tasked with going after Noriega and his chief supporters. The job of others was to take control of the main airport.

Seizing the airport required the use of a wide range of special ops weapons, gear, and tactics. First among them was close air support. On December 20, 1989, under cover of darkness, a squadron of AC-130 Spectre gunships approached the airport. Some of the planes flew in low. Unleashing the fury of machine guns and missiles, they blasted bunkers containing some of Noriega's defense forces.

Soldiers parachute from a C-130E Hercules aircraft into a drop zone to conduct operations in support of Operation Just Cause, the code name for the U.S. incursion into Panama in 1989.

Other gunships came in higher up and let loose a rain of Rangers. Plummeting downward, they opened their parachutes at a preplanned altitude and floated toward the airfield. One of the descending Rangers, T. Scott McGee, later recalled:

> It was real dark, almost black except for where [a] Spectre was shifting fire. I could see a trace of red light in my left peripheral vision where the AC-130 was smoking one last bunker. Looked kind of like a god throwing down a lightning bolt. Glad they were on our side!

An air-to-air left front view of a United States Air Force AC-130 Hercules aircraft during target practice

FIREFIGHT IN THE MEN'S ROOM

After the Rangers landed and cut loose their chutes, they swarmed into the airport terminal. There they saw a few hundred civilians waiting for commercial flights to arrive. Some of the commandos herded the concerned civilians into a side area to keep them safe.

Even as this was happening, other Rangers searched a nearby hangar. They found twenty Panamanian air force personnel hiding inside. Raising their M4 assault rifles, the commandos ordered the Panamanians to surrender at once. Faced with certain death, they did so.

Meanwhile, the Americans suspected that some of Noriega's soldiers might be hiding inside the terminal. That posed the threat of a sudden ambush. So the Rangers started searching. Armed with M4s and M9 pistols, two of them entered one of the airport's large men's rooms.

Sure enough, there were enemy fighters inside. Two of them leaped from a toilet stall and opened fire on the Rangers. This initiated a firefight, or battle involving firearms. One of the Americans was injured, but several more ran in and pulled him to safety. As they did so, two Panamanian pistol rounds struck one of the rescuers in the back of the head. At that moment he was thankful for his Kevlar helmet, which had stopped both bullets.

Once all of the Rangers had exited the men's room, one of them tossed an M67 hand-grenade inside. Under normal circumstances the explosion would have killed the enemy soldiers. In this case, however, the Panamanians were protected by the stalls' metal walls.

Several Rangers now reentered the men's room. Well-placed shots from their M4s bounced beneath the stalls, forcing the remaining enemy fighters out into the open. If the Panamanians had dropped their weapons, the commandos would have spared them. But the enemy soldiers chose to continue firing, so the Rangers killed them.

MERELY TOOLS

This small but hair-raising battle in the men's room counted for only a small part of the struggle for the airport. Other firefights erupted in different sectors of the terminal. Victorious in all of them, the U.S. commandos captured the entire facility in fewer than three hours. Much of this success was due to a varied array of weapons and equipment. Flying gunships, machine guns, missiles, parachutes, rifles, pistols, protective armor, grenades, and many others played their roles.

In the end, however, the weapons and equipment did not act alone. They were merely tools. And they were only as good as the people who wielded them. The commandos' skills, training, and courage combined to make the application of those tools efficient. Ranger McGee later proudly said that the special ops warriors "exemplify what is good about being an American. They are intelligent, well trained, motivated, and selfless in their devotion to duty. I am proud to have once been a member of their ranks."

Soldiers during
Operation Just Cause

fact BOX

Noriega on Trial

Manuel Noriega

During the invasion of Panama, Manuel Noriega was captured by U.S. commandos. He stood trial in the United States on a charge of racketeering (running a criminal operation). In 1992 he received a sentence of fifteen years in prison, which he served.

Noriega is escorted onto a U.S. Air Force aircraft by agents from the U.S. Drug Enforcement Agency.

Special Boat Team 22 demonstrates waterborne operations of their new Special Operations Craft-Riverine at the John C. Stennis Space Center in Hancock County, Mississippi.

Source Notes

Chapter 1: Deadly Handheld Weapons

p. 11,   "Rainey followed on foot . . ." Linda Robinson, *Masters of Chaos: The Secret History of the Special Forces* (New York: Public Affairs, 2004), 265.

p. 16,   "Humans are more . . ." Ibid., 2.

Chapter 2: Devices that Go Boom!

p. 20,   "are nothing more . . ." Rod Powers, "United States Military Weapons of War," http://usmilitary.about.com/od/armyweapons/l/aainfantry2.htm.

p. 22,   "designed to deliver . . ." "MK 19-3 40mm Grenade Machine Gun," U.S. Army, http://www.army.mil/factfiles/equipment/individual/mk193.html.

p. 25,   "The Stinger is a true . . ." Powers, "United States Military Weapons of War."

Chapter 3: Valuable Close Air Support

p. 32,   "The pilots took . . ." Dick Couch, *Down Range: Navy SEALs in the War on Terrorism* (New York: Three Rivers Press, 2005), 77.

p. 34,   "As the only close . . ." Rod Powers, "Air Force Fact Sheets: AC-130H Spectre," http://usmilitary.about.com/library/milinfo/affacts/blac-130hspectre.htm/.

Chapter 4: Assault and Survival Gear

p. 40,   "Camouflage material . . ." Tom Harris, "How Military Camouflage Works," http://science.howstuffworks.com/military-camouflage1.htm.

p. 43,   "GPS uses a collection . . ." Fred J. Pushies, *Special Ops: America's Elite Forces in 21st Century Combat* (St. Paul: MBI, 2003), 56.

p. 44,   "The devices are sensitive . . ." Powers, "United States Military Weapons of War."

p. 46,   "I am an American . . ." "Special Forces Creed," Special Forces, Green Berets, http://sfalx.com/h_sf_creed.htm.

Chapter 5: Special Ops Weapons in Action

p. 52,   "It was real dark . . ." Mir Bahmanyar, ed., "Personal Accounts from Torijos Tocumen Airfield Seizure," http://www.suasponte. com/m_torrijos.htm.

p. 54,   "exemplify what is good . . ." Ibid.

Glossary

armored vehicles: Jeeps, humvees, tanks, or other vehicles that have been fitted with protective sheets of metal.

beret: A small cloth cap worn by members of the Army Special Forces.

C4 (or plastique): A highly destructive explosive substance.

camouflage: Patterns and colors designed to make military uniforms, gear, and weapons blend in with a given natural setting.

civilian: A person who is not in the armed forces.

close air support: Aid given to ground fighters by planes and helicopters.

commando: An elite, specially trained soldier who is assigned to difficult, dangerous missions; or a special ops fighter.

firefight: A battle involving firearms.

GPS (Global Positioning System): A network of orbiting satellites that allow people to quickly compute their exact position on Earth's surface.

Kevlar: A rugged cloth-like material that is five times stronger than steel.

magazine (or clip): A small container inside a gun that holds the bullets.

police action: An attack or invasion made by one country against another to stop supposed crimes or other illegal activities.

psychological: Having to do with the human mind.

rappelling: Gliding downward along a vertical surface with the aid of ropes and pulleys.

round: A bullet or other projectile fired from a gun.

solar panels: Sheets containing large numbers of small cells that convert sunlight into electrical energy.

special ops: Short for Special Operations Forces (SOF), consisting of the U.S. military's elite units of soldiers; or commandos.

STAR (Surface to Air Recovery system): An array of devices aboard an aircraft that allow it to scoop up a person on the ground while the craft is still moving through the air.

weapons of mass destruction (WMDs): Weapons that cause large numbers of casualties, usually including nuclear, chemical, and biological devices.

Bibliography

Byrne, John A. "My Story: From an Army Ranger in Iraq to Harvard." http://poetsandquants.com/2010/08/18/my-story-from-an-army-ranger-in-iraq-to-harvard/.

Cooke, Tim. *U.S. Army Special Forces*. New York: Powerkids Press, 2012.

Couch, Dick. *Down Range: Navy SEALs in the War on Terrorism*. New York: Three Rivers Press, 2005.

Labrecque, Ellen. *Special Forces*. Mankrato, MN: Heinemann-Raintree, 2012.

Mann, Don. *Inside SEAL Team Six: My Life and Missions with America's Elite Warriors*. New York: Little Brown, 2011.

Montana, Jack. *Navy Seals*. Broomall, PA: Mason Crest, 2011.

Nagle, Jeanne. *Delta Force*. New York: Gareth Stevens, 2012.

Nelson, Drew. *Green Berets*. New York: Gareth Stevens, 2012.

Pushies, Fred J. *Special Ops: America's Elite Forces in 21st Century Combat*. St. Paul: MBI, 2003.

Robinson, Linda. *Masters of Chaos: The Secret History of the Special Forces*. New York: Public Affairs, 2004.

Sandler, Michael. *Army Rangers in Action*. New York: Bearport, 2008.

———. *Pararescumen in Action*. New York: Bearport, 2008.

Web sites

Army Enhanced Night Vision Goggles
http://www.army.mil/article/18980/army-fielding-enhanced-night-vision-goggles/

Army Special Forces Center
http://www.military.com/army-special-forces/training.html

Defense Industry Daily. "The USA's M4 Carbine Controversy."
http://www.defenseindustrydaily.com/the-usas-m4-carbine-controversy-03289/

How Stuff Works. "How the Army Rangers Work."
http://science.howstuffworks.com/army-ranger5.htm

Official Web site of the Navy SEALs and SWCC
http://www.sealswcc.com/

U.S. Air Force. Fact Sheet for the AC-130 Spectre Gunship
http://www.af.mil/information/factsheets/factsheet.asp?fsID=71

U.S. Air Force. Fact Sheet for the CV-22 Osprey
http://www.af.mil/information/factsheets/factsheet.asp?fsID=3668

U.S. Air Force. Pararescue. "Superman School."
http://www.pararescue.com/unitinfo.aspx?id=490

Weapons of the Special Forces
http://www.popularmechanics.com/technology/military/1281576

Index

Photo Credits